MW00913168

A Janitor's Book of Poems

By

Colin Zarhett

© 2001 by Colin Zarhett. All rights reserved.

No part of this book may be reproduced, stored in a retrieval
system, or transmitted by any means, electronic, mechanical,
photocopying, recording, or otherwise, without written
permission from the author.

ISBN: 0-75966-343-2

This book is printed on acid free paper.

1stBooks – rev. 10/01/01

Oct 2002

DEDICATED TO THE STECIK WOMEN

Joni

I hope you enjoy this book of poems. It was written by a high school friend of my Arthur Zartko later known as colin.

Friend always

Teri

iii

Kovalcin

DAD

I can still see his eyes as if it were yesterday

DAD

I waved good-bye until the next time

DAD

Death stole from me—

and my heart still bears a hole

I will never forget my Dad's face—

implanted in my memory forever.

Daily I'm reminded how my life used to be

DAD

Still wanting my life to be how it once was

My Dad gave me a sense of belonging

gave me a special place in his life

I frequently wonder how my life would have been—

had he lived

MY DAD

1

Colin Zarhett

THE LAST DANCE

When the last dance is danced

Life's mystery is still sweet

With every step to kingdom come

The old always make room for the new—

that's the key

With every breath I take

I give thanks to God above

In my paginating reality

Is there a place for you and me?

Among the rivers to the sea!

Colin Zarhett

THAT DAY

It was the day we realized

all of the hurts of yesterday

that we buried in long lost dreams

THAT DAY-it collapsed inward

on itself-insomnia gripped

our minds-the face I wear

is not mine...but I still have

my name. I had hope as I

looked through the windows of

your soul. I did my best to

see the person you were trying

to hide

Hoping that person was human

...maybe just like me. THAT DAY...

all the hurts...yesterday

Colin Zarhett

INDIANA STREET

The broom handle smashed the ball

sending it straight in the air down

Indiana Street

My Nike's loose tongues hanging

carried me over first base

(Mrs. Tomchuk's broken flower pot)

zipping around second base

(the sewer lid)

past third base

(A flattened Kotex box)

and a foto finish to home plate

(Dizzy Denny's math book)

I copped a drag

on Pupa's Camel the guys all told me

I should be playing for the Pirates

Marlene Bartko came over and

told me my fly was open

7

Colin Zarhett

ASI ES LA VIDA

The crying of new babies... the laughter of pre-schoolers

The knowledge of teenagers... the complexities of adulthood

The sun in it's zenith... the wisdom of age... the humor of it all

The understanding of a leaf... the moon on the new fallen snow

asi es la vida...such is life...

Colin Zarhett

YOU LEARN

That you

can endure-

and that you have

worth-

and you learn-

with every

good-bye-

you learn.

Colin Zarhett

A TALE OF JOAN

I seek

a peaceful violence

subtle disturbance

quiet noise

artful enchantment

glowing darkness

Colin Zarhett

THE MORNING NEWSPAPER

You've been gone a long while—
what we had together no one else could have—
the music plays on, and the damage is done—
I was the one who said it wouldn't last forever
then again it was I who laughed the loudest
as the wind chased us on those long walks—
The early mornings—only you and I—
staring in the store windows
There was anticipation and expectation
dreaming far away dreams—
The night turn waitress who told us
about her alky husband and all of her seven kids—
Marge was her name—I think—
The paper guy—remember—he gave us cups of
steaming hot chocolate—as the snow decorated us—
The creaky bed—steamy windows—I asked nothing—
now you're gone—and here I am—by myself—alone!!
and my soul is stranded on an island full of sorrow

Colin Zarhett

IT'S SUMMER

Please that part of you that is still a kid

Take a walk in the woods, enjoy the fragrances of the wildflowers

Watch a butterfly flutter past you and marvel at it's color

Dip your toes in a clear stream

Please that part of you that's still a kid

Take a drive in the country and breathe all of the country smells

See the sunrise with someone you love

Tip toe through the tulips and kiss your pretty girl's lips

Enjoy far away church bells chiming

Please that part of you that is still a kid!!!

Colin Zarhett

PRIVATE MOMENTS

A daughter lying on the bed, arms stretching, out to you

Arched eyebrows, red lips open, eyes needing you

Flimsy negligee

Curves and angles exposed

Buttocks exposed, thin waist ends beneath her breasts

Creamy white skin—desire glowing

Fulfill fantasy in opulent flesh

Get up-and-

hand her the money

Colin Zarhett

I BOUGHT MY LOVE

Room always hot

    radiator clanging-hissing

        I asked nothing-gave less

            you are gone

                now-tonight I thought of you

                    as I read my $1.00 worth of love

                        the Sunday newspaper

                            I bought earlier this evening

                              Saturday!

Colin Zarhett

TWO WORLDS

I looked back upon the past

What it was when I left

I thought about the future?

Except another season of the past

...what is the past? except the

never changing season.

The memory I can't abide!!

Should I run and hide??

Breathless and heaving from the

past I find so displeasing (it has

to be said) I can't run from

the constant threat of the never

changing season-a season without

form, rhythm, or reason.

Colin Zarhett

TIME#11

Now it is the second

First it is a demand

Then it is a command

Finity is a strange land

*and...*WINTER CAME

Green trees of summer
burgeoned around us

You won my heart when
you held my hand

Your voice full of
love's sweet art

Grass full and soft as silk
Air as sweet as mother's milk

A bird singing in my far off dream-
his song sounding through sunlight's beam

The truth—my heart
hardly slowed its beat

My thoughts raced far ahead of me
Dreaming of joys not to be

The winds blew cold as winter came
and froze my bold, youthful passion cruelly.

Colin Zarhett

ALICE MAKES THE WRONG TURN

Cracks occur

without notice

Irregular jagged edges

razor fine

expose the black further

Does she fine the madhatter?

They're wide enough

to fall into—maybe Alice

will find the hare

Colin Zarhett

THE BALLOON IN THE PARK

I woke up today-and how time has slipped away
Suddenly Mom it's hard to find the memories
Shadowy misty yesteryear
The laughter and the tears

The balloon flew away from me in the park

The good times and the bad and all the others in between
Reaching back for the joy and sorrows-
I put them away in my mind

The balloon flew away from me that day in the park

You borrow memories of time to spend for tomorrow
Remember, I shall always remember you, Mom

The balloon flew high in the blue sky!!!

Colin Zarhett

THE DAY BOB DIED

His wife Kathleen cried

so she made a promise

as she wrote a *to do* list

that no matter how near

or no matter how far

Wherever you are—

I shall love you.

You let me share your life

first as your friend and then as your wife.

Thank you for all of the seasons

of knowing you for ten years.

For you—there will always be my silent tears.

Colin Zarhett

NAKED IN THE RAIN

I stand deep in icy waters
because the revelation of truth is
concealed. The mask of the hidden
past must be knocked away

I saw the rain fall on it, and
each tear of rain with its own
destination and history helped wipe
the mask away.

A phantom murmur brushes past
my elbow. Her voice
in my ear banishes my fright.
For some sweet moments we are
two murmurs. The words you
whispered made my love turn cold.
I never want to feel that pain again.

Colin Zarhett

Me And Dreams

Come

while I sleep and dream
late at night

Longing to see the changing tide.

Account dreams are the wishes
of an innocent heart.

Just a moment of sweet reverie.

Searching for the *giver* of dreams

Because everything seems to be
going wrong.

But the brightness of the lazy
moon shining over the glistening
lake encourages me to keep
looking for the *mender* of all
things broken.

Colin Zarhett

A NEW DAWN

Going forward is the only goal

I understand the metaphysics
of nature

No doubt in all of nature's things
there is a pattern and beauty
in the harmony of the eternal
cycle of life.

Always trying to
gather the touch of the sun's rays in this life.

Always dreaming the dreams of
a forsaken life that
knowing fingers have touched, caressed
and remembered.

Sometimes I sit outside and watch
the trees and looking out over a
field of flowers drifting along on
a summer breeze.

I look one way and travel
another.

Colin Zarhett

AWAKENINGS

Spring
   Sun
      Blue Skies
      Robins
         Budding Green Trees
         Butterflies
         Flowers
            Imagination
            New Dreams

Colin Zarhett

THE BENCH

He's sitting on a bench in the park
a bag of peanuts for the noisy, chattering squirrels-
He's looking at the sky
maybe he'll stay until dark-
This guy with heavy beard growth and no words
only gestures for the quick squirrels-
A tarnished knight in today's society?
Mid sixties and no-shine shoes.
His family-where are they?
Could he be a lost uncle of mine?
I would be embarrassed to claim him a family member
my musing is interrupted-
A black limo is slowing down where he is sitting.
He smiles as he enters the limo
he departs-
My only thought-
first impressions do they really count?

Colin Zarhett

BRADDOCK

A mosaic of houses

on hillsides

like tombstones

struck with sunlight

Colin Zarhett

FOR BEVERLY JEAN

A warm summer's night

the top of a dark lonely hill

Gentle rain—a soft wind

I walk among the sleeping trees and flowers

Rain caresses me—and peace consumes me

I am what I am—me

Colin Zarhett

A TALE OF JOAN

I seek a peaceful violence

subtle disturbance

quiet noise

artful enchantment

glowing darkness

Colin Zarhett

THE CROW IN THE CANYON

Soaring gracefully above the cliffs

A free spirit drifts

He lands—our eyes meet

There is a stillness oh so sweet

He walks with me along the trail

I speak to him softly—he does not flail

For a few minutes we are one

In the shadow of the morning sun

Man and nature both in tune

in this Grand Canyon

He flies off

and now part of me is flying with abandon

Colin Zarhett

WALLYWORLD

Hundreds of faces of different races

Young and old

joining the river of time's race

Some faces were like old lace

Magic Kingdom, Epcot

It was a keen battle of strollers

From all of creation's corners

Animal Kingdom—there was hundreds of babies

in strollers

Mom—Dad—pushing and talking

Colin Zarhett

SWEET DREAMS

The whispering wind in the cool summer night

Somewhere between here and there

Cabbages are green

Watermelons are, too!

I woke the next morning kind of blue

I thought of you—and—

I knew the Blue Bird of Happiness

wouldn't crap in my left shoe

Colin Zarhett

FIREPLACE

When the night gets cold—I sit in front of the fireplace and wrap my memories tight around me. In the glow of the fire, I drift off to sleep and long ago memories are there quickly. The fun we had at our Las Vegas wedding. The vacations in Hawaii — the sunsets. How we danced the night on one of your birthdays. The dinners you made with your love. The Masonic Ball we attended—we were the talk of the evening. Can you believe it? I don't know where the times have gone. Thank you for the special parts of my heart—that I can't give to anyone else.

Colin Zarhett

THE FIRE TRUCK HAS A FLAT TIRE

I never knew it could be like it was...when you

held me in your hands like a bunch of flowers...my

world was simply one...loving you it seemed the

the thing to do...vividly you laughter rings in my

ears...your smile, your dancing eyes...a memory

only I could cherish...simple, sweet and so

pure...why didn't I give more...this I'll never

know...the park...the swings...the old red

fire truck...it's gone now...an apartment house

is there...shiny windows, quaint balconies...sort

of profane isn't it...because I loved you best in the

park...and you never knew

Colin Zarhett

A BROKEN GATE-A BROKEN HEART

I should have known something was wrong-
You spilled the coffee at breakfast-
When I left for work the hinges fell off the front gate-
I cursed adamantly-
I should have gone back and told you how much I love you-
But you told me last night *the party's over sweetheart-*
I just laughed and smoked another joint-
You went to take a bath-
It was a cold dark autumn night-
Feeling small I drifted off to sleep-
Such dreams-
Our first kiss, our first love making-
Fantasy-joy- most of all you and me-
It's dark now as I walk through the front door-
I knew something was wrong-
I read your note-
Something funny happened-
A tear of mine fell on the paper-
Blotting out your word *love-*
Odd-no not really-
It's you that's lonely now

GEMINI LOVE

I like it when you're near me

you make me feel new—

Shining as the the silvered morning dew

I like the feel of you—

and—no matter what we do or say-

In the early light we get up

and go our separate way

and gamble #13 twice plus eleven

on a given day

Colin Zarhett

CHASING GHOSTS

No reason—no rhyme. The roads were full of slush and slime...

The restless trees were bending and waving their limbs... My heart was

beating faster on that bizarre night...Rustling leaves were twisting and twirling

in my sight...Pounding rain in twisting sheets and the windshield wipers didn't

wipe the rain fast enough...As I turned up my street—suddenly there was a

star shining brightly. Quickly I turned off the engine—closing the garage door...

The trees swayed in voodoo rhythm and the winds kissed my cheeks as I opened

the back door to my house...I was home...

Colin Zarhett

GLADA

Kathie clapped for the clown—

I cried—his funny nose fell off—

this poem is for my new friend—

A friend to treasure until time's end

She keeps the violets always blue—

Kathie makes you want to do—

and this is good—when you are down—

Kathie claps for the clown—you feel good—

as you should—even though you just

might slip in a pile of elephant poop.

Makes you want to get back up—

look around—not hurt (only self pride)

The music within my heart filled the air...

Smile and clap for the clown!

Colin Zarhett

A LONG GOODBYE

A fireplace—flames burning

now dim—flickers and fade—

falling into darkness—

Are they gone?

Stars slip from sight—

No! they come back

struggling to be—

and— I believe with you beside me

our life will be full

Colin Zarhett

I'M YOURS

My love

forever I will be yours

Never betraying your trust

Always loving you until all of time

The soft winds whisper

My love

The night mist was all around

Then it settled

In the misty remembrances of my dreams

Colin Zarhett

MIRTHLESS LAUGH

My Father,
what was left of the man
lay in a state of clutter
flowers and people

I sat quietly
memorizing his features
an all out effort to defend my sanity.

Some of these sympathizers
didn't recognize his existence.
Now my Dad was without voice, temper, opinions
and devoid of pride.

People must have felt a cathartic need
to pay their last and only respects.

Later
I kissed my Father a last time
and gently closed the coffin
I swear I heard a soft mirthless laugh.

Colin Zarhett

Liz

If you like me

like I like you

everything is swell

because if you like me

like I like you-

that's being a friend

Colin Zarhett

STREET LULLABY

Stay away from that black girl—Red

See

Ain't your turf

See

You here to cop smack not my woman

See

The stars fade out—she ain't for sale

See

Your money—buys something—

not everything

Let my woman be.

Colin Zarhett

MARCHING

What is today?

I marched on and on

To a different drummer

That makes me different

Drowning out my senses

The cacophony of sounds

I see fine detail in simplicity

What is tomorrow?

That will make me the same

I march a fine line between the earth and the sky

What was yesterday?

That made me so strange—and—people marching through

superficial lifestyles into nonentity

Colin Zarhett

EVERY OLD MAN'S SONG

Maybe I should have smiled

   When she smiled so sweetly at me

      Maybe I should not have let clouds of jealousy

      float around in my mind

         Maybe—just maybe her love for me

         wouldn't have fragmented

            Maybe I should not have let

those love moments be so hard to find

   Maybe I should have said I love you a ton of times

   Maybe she wouldn't have left my arms

      Maybe when I was young in my thoughts—

   maybe just maybe she'd still be mine

Colin Zarhett

MEL

This is for my friend Mel

One day he was walking through

a dell and came upon a well

in the middle of this dell

Pray tell said he —I thirst

In an eye's wink he fell down this evil well

You know—my friend Mel

is still at the bottom of the well

hollering like hell above the clanging of the bell

on top of the well in the middle of the dell

Time will tell

The tolling of the bell

The dried up well—and—

Mel is gone for now

I AM WHO I AM -ME

Bits and pieces of memories

Mental snapshots of memories

Long ago childhood memories

dreamlike memories

Whirling fast memories

Frozen in time memories

Some memories—no reason or rhyme

Symphonic collage of memories

Mindful memories

That I am who I am—me

Colin Zarhett

MYSELF

One word with 10,000 meanings—LOVE

The timeless awakening dawn's light—

You lay there on your side—

Face forward in a halo of golden hair—

You are the light that illuminates my reality—

I love when we are one—

The empty champagne bottle—

our clothes scattered about the room—

I loved it—you and me—

with all the voices of the wind talking

I didn't mean to tear the Valentine up—

I couldn't understand why you'd want to leave me—

I love you with my heart, my soul—

I am lost in the reflection of another dimension

Colin Zarhett

MOUNT CHARLESTON CROW

Abundant sunlight—A mountain's majesty
Sitting there—on the mountain—it seemed so right
Enjoying the beauty —I was in awe of the mountain

A slight noise—I turned quickly—the crow fluttered his wings,
Our eyes met as he squawked—he landed to my right.
His stance was majestic—I moved toward him.
He took off—gracefully flapping his wings—soaring high
above— then—
swooped into a tree. He sat on the a limb fluttering his wings—
his gold eyes looking straight into mine. He cawed a couple of
times.
With a flutter of wings he flew off.

MY BROTHER

I can't believe how fast
time goes—and—
Why things happen—only
God knows
What is this thing—life—
that is so tumultuous
Life is like a rain
cloud—unpredictable and
confusing

You are my brother

Looking thru the windows
of your soul—you are a
person like me—Perhaps—
a little human like me

My brother

The new hope we feel
at each morning
As the night darkness
gives way to first light

You are my brother

The depths of the great
and mighty oceans
Clouds ever soft
drifting by
I've met success
and defeat
Happiness and Sorrow
What might have been
—and forever lost—

Colin Zarhett

Only time will show the cost
As winter's twilight begins
the moon reflects the
sunset from its breast
and the clouds offer
the moon no place to hide—

You are my brother

MY MARY

As I stumble thru this life—you—*My Mary* are there

You know—Mary—the cruelest ironies of life

are consecrated with the passage of time—

Yet you are there to pick me up in the world—

My Mary I love you—

even though solitude is my guide in my life—and—

my memories are trapped in time—

Your words keep me alive—*My Mary*

Though I often speak in riddles—

with the night as my companion

I cross a thousand lifetimes—to love you—*My Mary*

Colin Zarhett

NICK

He was my father. I am at my lifetime
as he was when he passed.

I wonder if he often struggled—like a
desert flower—alone—in the
life sand's of deception.

I wonder if it made him strong through
the joy—pain—sorrow??? Believe
it or not in 1998, I see in my dreams
a new hope.

I wonder if as Nick was growing old—
if he remembered the ones who loved him.
Ultimately true feelings look and listen
to where one sees

I wonder if Nick was scared of the
closeness he put away in his lifetime.
Nick what has time done? Eyes dimmed,
shoulder bowed from all the hard work.
Thirty years ago it all seemed so clear—
Now it is my turn to walk the *rock
strewn dusty road.*

Colin Zarhett

COMING AND GOING

The lady with the old dried apple face sat rocking

in her dress of lace

surrounded by merry shouts

People coming and going

Strangers are the only ones

who visit *old age homes* before the holidays

not during

Colin Zarhett

There Was Always Time

An old man alone—with his thoughts

It's awful to leave him with millions of stars of the night-

and-the days of winter lace

*One can't call back the seconds, minutes, and the hours of the
time race*

When you love someone you must tell them

or the moment passes you by

There was always time ahead of me

The years have passed so quickly

It was only yesterday-it seems anyway-

that you and I were searching for a way to make our life better

but we moved in unstilled waters full of animus, ache, and pain

that even new rain couldn't wash away

Colin Zarhett

A PLACE

I know a place

where I want to go

Because of the quiet

fresh fallen snow

Because of sounds—only fresh

flowers opening in bloom

The guardian of all—the man

in the moon

The owl ever so quiet

no movement—just his refrains

The falling of new gentle rain

A delightful aroma

that conquers the senses

Yes, I'm just buying time!!

Colin Zarhett

SO PRETTY

A spring day—a field

the tall grass brushes against my legs as I walk

Look—a flower

the stem is broken

I hold it in my hand

so pretty—yet—

soon it will die

MY RED HEAD

Even if you do mismatch my socks and wear my tee shirts to the laundry
Loving you...

Or when you hang your stockings to dry in the bathroom
Loving you...

And when your moods are like the changing shoreline of the sea
Loving you...

Loving you is the right thing to do...

Or in the morning when you hair lay

on the pillow like the sleepy golden new day
Loving you...

Loving you my Red head...

When you smile and

sleepily ask if it's time to go
Loving you...

As you kiss me lightly on the forehead and dash off to work

Somehow I know that loving you is the right thing to do...

As you cook our dinner and tell me about your day, cheerfully chattering away

Suddenly you shyly smile and ask me...if I've had a nice day

Colin Zarhett

Loving you...

As the wind of the day has quietly gone by us...there is just you and me

We go to a place...a place where no one else will ever go

Loving you is the right thing to do, my Red Head

SANDCASTLE

Beach

Sand

Water

Imagination

Kingdom of your mind

Colin Zarhett

SCORPIO

Relentless time—spring buds opening for the first and last time

even though all I have is today

As I sit inside my emotional cave

Gone are yesterdays dreams—

what about tomorrow's sorrow?

I don't know

With my imagination as my only guide—

on and on I go

For I see in you today, tomorrow, and yesterday

For all I know is loyalty...and

There is nothing so whole as a broken heart!

A SIMPLE GESTURE

The scent from your hug still lingers

My thoughts are interrupted

Again I feel your warmth

Your embrace-your fingers

pressed against my back

Your hair softly against my cheek

Pleasurable insanity

Contented-a simple gesture

That means so much

Colin Zarhett

UNUSUAL THINGS

Things that go bump in

the night

Today they're operating

during daylight

Don't get full of fright

Because they're nothing but

the usual—Witches,

Goblins, and Ghosts

working daylight

TWISTED AND TANGLED

In the movie of my life

I took for granted—my shadow

the walls were alive—with my shadow

My arms were twisted and tangled

My screams bounced off the walls

Desperately I wanted to escape to reality

My life—THEY—said I wasn't strong enough

My soul remains twisted

in the movie of my life!

Colin Zarhett

WRINKLED SKIN AND THINNING HAIR

I hear the river rushing *as I walk alone*

I look for reflections of what not only *surrounds* but is also *within*

It is a longing desire to *feel satisfied*

In my past I never thought about wrinkled skin and thinning hair

As I sit and think of you

The color of the night sky is—*longing*

The agony of love is—*longing*

Colin Zarhett